SATAN'S STRATEGY, GOD'S REMEDY

An Important Message

From

An Ancient Document

About the author

Boon-Sing Poh was born in Malaysia in 1954. Brought up in a pagan background, he was saved by God's grace through faith in Jesus Christ while studying in the United Kingdom. He returned to Malaysia to become a lecturer in a university for six years, founded the first Reformed Baptist Church in the country in 1983, and was imprisoned for his faith from 1987 to 1988 for a period of 325 days. He is the pastor of Damansara Reformed Baptist Church (DRBC) in Kuala Lumpur, a contented husband, a thankful father of four sons, and a happy grandfather. He earned the PhD degree in Electronics Engineering from the University of Liverpool, UK, the Diploma in Religious Study from Cambridge University, UK, and the PhD degree in Theology from North-West University, SA.

SATAN'S STRATEGY, GOD'S REMEDY

An Important Message

From

An Ancient Document

BOON-SING POH

Published by

Good News Enterprise

Contents

To The Reader   vii

1   The Message Of Genesis 3   7

    1.1   Our Roots Revealed   8

    1.2   Our Current Status Revealed   13

    1.3   The Way Ahead Revealed   16

2   Satan's Strategy   19

    2.1   Catching You Unaware   20

    2.2   Attacks Indirectly   24

    2.3   Questions The Word   28

    2.4   Appeals To The Carnal Senses . . .   31

3   Man's Folly   35

    3.1   Desiring Forbidden Knowledge . .   36

    3.2   Attempting To Cover Yourself . . .   42

CONTENTS

3.3   Hiding From God 44

3.4   Doubting God's Solution 48

4   God's Remedy   51

4.1   Exposing Your Sins 52

4.2   Exposing Your Useless Efforts . . . 55

4.3   Exposing You To His Solution . . . 58

4.4   Exposing Satan's Desire To Destroy

You 62

5   Over To You!   67

To The Reader

Tipping points do occur in life. A small change can tip the balance of one's life and bring about a big change – for better or for worse. While tipping points are attributed to chance or fate by most people, the Bible teaches that God sovereignly controls all events. Furthermore, God desires all men to be saved and to come to the knowledge of the truth.

Found in the Bible is an ancient document, namely Genesis 3:1-21, which bears an important message for us all. It is part of a larger book which is often neglected because of its antiquity. We do well to at least pay attention to the message of Genesis 3:1-21, for it might just be the tipping point to your life, for good. Please read through this booklet which attempts to bring out that message.

With best wishes,

Boon-Sing Poh,
Kuala Lumpur, 2020.

Genesis 3:1-21

1 Now the serpent was more cunning than any beast of the field which the Lord God had made. And he said to the woman, "Has God indeed said, 'You shall not eat of every tree of the garden'?"

2 And the woman said to the serpent, "We may eat the fruit of the trees of the garden;

3 but of the fruit of the tree which is in the midst of the garden, God has said, 'You shall not eat it, nor shall you touch it, lest you die.'"

4 Then the serpent said to the woman, "You shall not surely die.

5 For God knows that in the day you eat of it your eyes will be opened, and you will be like God, knowing good and evil."

6 So when die woman saw that the tree was good for food, that it was pleasant to the eyes, and a tree desirable to make one wise, she took of its fruit and ate. She also gave to her husband with her, and he ate.

7 Then the eyes of both of them were opened, and they knew that they were naked; and they sewed fig leaves together and made themselves coverings.

8 And they heard the sound of the Lord God walking in the garden in the cool of the day, and Adam and his wife hid them-

selves from the presence of the
Lord God among the trees of
the garden.

9 Then the Lord God called to Adam
and said to him, "Where are
you?"

10 So he said, "I heard Your voice in
the garden, and I was afraid
because I was naked; and I hid
myself."

11 And He said, "Who told you that
you were naked? Have you eaten
from the tree of which I commanded you that you should
not eat?"

12 Then the man said, "The woman
whom You gave to be with me,
she gave me of the tree, and I
ate."

13 And the Lord God said to the woman, "What is this you have done?" The woman said, "The serpent deceived me, and I ate."

14 So the Lord God said to the serpent: "Because you have done this, you are cursed more than all cattle, and more than every beast of the field; on your belly you shall go, and you shall eat dust all the days of your life.

15 And I will put enmity between you and the woman, and between your seed and her Seed; He shall bruise your head, and you shall bruise His heel."

16 To the woman He said: "I will greatly multiply your sorrow and your conception; in pain you shall bring forth children; your de-

sire shall be for your husband,
and he shall rule over you."

17 Then to Adam He said, "Because
you have heeded the voice of
your wife, and have eaten from
the tree of which I commanded
you, saying, 'You shall not eat
of it': Cursed is the ground for
your sake; in toil you shall eat
of it all the days of your life.

18 Both thorns and thistles it shall
bring forth for you, and you
shall eat the herb of the field.

19 In the sweat of your face you shall
eat bread till you return to the
ground, for out of it you were
taken; for dust you are, and to
dust you shall return."

20 And Adam called his wife's name

Eve, because she was the mother of all living.

6

21 Also for Adam and his wife the Lord God made tunics of skin, and clothed them.

One

The Message Of Genesis 3

Therefore, just as through one man sin entered the world, and death through sin, and thus death spread to all men, because all sinned... For as by one man's disobedience many were made sinners, so also by one Man's obedience many will be made righteous. (Romans 5:12,19)

There are many stories that revolve around the idea of finding a secret formula to produce a special cure for an otherwise incurable disease. Many of such stories have been produced into movie shows. We can think of examples like "Lorenzo's Oil", "Jungle Doctor", and so on. Many traditional Kung-fu stories run along a similar line. We have the hero who finds a long-lost manual that helps him achieve greater heights in his fighting skill, so that he is able to overcome a powerful villain.

We may look upon Genesis 3 as a document like that. It contains the story of what happened to our first parents in the Garden of Eden. It reveals to us the consequences of their fall from innocency. It gives us a special insight into our lives today. Put another way, Genesis 3 is of crucial importance to the understanding of our past, our present, and our future. It reveals to us our roots, our current status before God, and the key to our future stability and happiness.

1.1   Our Roots Revealed

We are all aware of the great importance of knowing our roots. Many young people grow up happily until a stage when they become troubled about their roots. An identity crisis occurs in them. They begin to ask who they are, where they are from, how they are to relate to the many people around them. This problem is more acute in our modern age in which there has been great mobility and migration of people. There are those who grow up in an environment in which are found people of diverse cultures and different colours of skin. I believe it is this crisis of identity that has given rise to the popularity of books tracing the ancestry of individuals, clans, or even whole ethnic groups.

You might claim that this is never a problem with you. But wait till your children grow up, and your daughter comes home one day to tell you that she is going to marry someone whose skin colour is totally different from yours! What would your reaction be? You might say that you are an open-minded person, that this would be no problem to you. But is that really true? Would you be willing to let your daughter marry him?

Would there be full consent from within your heart? And even if you have no racial prejudice of any kind, there is still the practical problems of having a son-in-law from a different culture, who speaks a different language, who eats different food... How should you view these differences? Would these things affect your relationship with him, and with your daughter? Should these be allowed to affect your relationship?

You would not have these kinds of problems if you understand that the human race is actually one. Mankind is actually one family! That is a fact. It can easily be proven. We all know that the tiger and the lion belong to the cat family. If you were to crossbreed a lion with a tiger, you would get a perfectly healthy offspring which has two eyes, two ears, one nose, one mouth, one heart, one stomach, and so on. You would get a complete animal which has nothing lacking in it. This has actually been done. The product has been called a 'liger', a cross between the lion and the tiger. You may do the same for a cow and a buffalo. That is because the cow and the buffalo belongs to the same family. However, if you were to cross-breed a tiger and a cow, you will never get a living creature of any kind. You may use artificial insemination, but you will never succeed in getting a living creature of any kind. The reason is that the tiger and the cow belong to two different families.

That is not the case with human beings. You can take the tallest and whitest European, and marry him to the shortest and blackest pigmy from central Africa, and you will produce a perfectly normal offspring. The reason is that the human race is actually one family. This confirms to us the truth taught in the Bible that mankind descended from the same pair of parents. God created all the creatures of the world "according to their kind", but he created only one pair of humans. We are all descended from Adam and Eve. Once you grasp this truth, you will no longer be too concerned about the differences of culture and the different colours of skin among people.

You suddenly realise that your roots stretch all the way to the very beginning, when God created the first humans.

Those who attempt to trace their ancestry can go back only five or six generations, and no more. They can perhaps trace their ancestry to a certain village in Swatow in China, or to a village in Kerala, India. But they are unable to go further back. This exercise of tracing their ancestry may give them a certain sense of satisfaction, but it still does not account for their origin. Genesis 3, however, snows that all of us originated from the same parents. There is our ultimate satisfaction! We know where the whole human race comes from. We are able to comprehend the history of mankind at one sweep, even if we do not know all the events that have transpired during the time in between.

1.2   Our Current Status Revealed

A knowledge of our roots gives a certain stability to our lives. It shows us where we came from. But it also explains why we are what we are today. It reveals to us that we stand guilty before God because of the sin of our first parents. We are guilty in two ways. First, we share in the guilt of Adam. God made Adam the head of the human race. He stood in our place. We were "in him" when he sinned against God. You may not like the idea. You might protest that you did not have a choice in the sin of Adam. You may protest as much as you like, but the fact remains that you are held guilty by God for Adam's sin. We see this principle operating in many areas of life. Consider this example. If the Prime Minister of our nation were to declare war on, say, Japan, none of the citizens in this country may say that he is not at war. You might go to Japan and say to the people there that you are only a tourist, and that you have nothing to do with the war. But will the Japanese listen to you? Before you know it, you will be held as a prisoner of war! That is because all the citizens of this country are linked to the Prime Minister by virtue of the fact that he is our representative head. In the same way, Adam was the representative head of the human race. When he sinned against God, and broke His commandment, we were all held guilty with him.

Not only are we held guilty by God, but we have the additional problem of the pollution of sin in our lives. Since all of us descended from Adam and Eve, we share in their fallen nature. Something happened to them when they rebelled against God and ate the fruit of the forbidden tree. Their nature became twisted and filthy. They knew guilt, and shame, and fear. They were now capable of lying, blaming others for their sins, and committing sins of various kinds. That sinful, polluted nature of theirs was passed down to their descendants. Since we are all descended from them, our nature is also twisted and filthy. That accounts for why it is that children naturally take to lying, stealing, and rebelling against their parents. You do not have to teach your children all these. They will show forth these sins as they grow up. These sins are not picked up from their environment. These sins come naturally to them. Your children may have been induced to show all these sins by the bad examples of others, but you have still to account for why it is that they should follow them at all. It is because they have a twisted and polluted nature! Even without the examples of others, your children will show forth these sins sooner than you expect.

Children do grow up. You are children who have grown up, are you not? All through the years, you have sinned in worse and worse ways! Your conscience testifies to the fact that you have done wrong towards God. You have broken His laws. You stand guilty before God for your sins! We are already guilty because of our first parents' sin. We now stand guilty before God for our own sins! Genesis 3 gives us the explanation for our predicament. It shows to us that we stand guilty before God, and God's holy anger now rests on us. We are enemies of God. Every time that we try to get near to God, we are repelled by the force of enmity which exists between the two parties. We cannot get near to Him, let alone be welcomed by Him, unless something is done to our situation. That is the big problem we are faced with!

1.3   The Way Ahead Revealed

Genesis 3 reveals to us our roots. It reveals to us our current condition and status before God. And it also reveals to us the way ahead. We know that left to ourselves, there will be no possibility of being reconciled to God. What is life if God does not smile on you? You live in His world. You enjoy His benefits. But you know that His holy anger rests on you everyday of your life!

Imagine yourself going to work each day and knowing that your boss is unhappy with you! It will not be long before you break under the burden of your guilt before God. That is why a lot of people are unhappy deep down in their hearts. They do not have a clear conscience before God. And if the burden of guilt, shame and fear does not break you, God will break you in due time. Your sins will catch up with you. Death will come to you. There is the judgment day that all of us will have to face. And after that what? You know that nothing good awaits you. Eternal separation from God, and from all that is good, awaits you. Sufferings of the worst kind await you. You will be plunged into darkness forever...

Thankfully, that is not all that is shown to us by Genesis 3. We are shown that there is the possibility of reconciliation with God. We are shown God's way of saving sinners. We are shown that a Saviour will be provided. Those of us who know something of the Bible's teaching would know that that Saviour is none other than the Lord Jesus Christ. The way ahead is revealed as bright for those who come to faith in Christ. Our sins may be cancelled! Our guilt may be lifted! We may gain a new status before God and be accepted by Him! All these are possible through the Saviour of the world, namely Jesus Christ. We know that life on this earth is so short, and temporary. We want to live out the remaining stretch of life well. We wish to live usefully, with a sense of purpose and well-being, and with the certainty that we are heading for better things ahead. All this is shown to be possible only through the Saviour whom God has provided, namely Jesus Christ. His death on the cross, and His resurrection, have secured all this for His people.

These, then, are the unique features of Genesis 3. Our past, our present, and our future are revealed to us. We may gain a better understanding of ourselves, and know how best to live. These truths form the outline of Genesis 3. We must now consider the details.

Two

Satan's Strategy

Now the serpent was more cunning than any beast of the field which the Lord God had made. And he said to the woman, "Has God indeed said, 'You shall not eat of every tree of the garden'?" (Genesis 3:1)

A Kung-fu manual must be valued and studied closely. The formula for the precious medicine must be scrutinised and understood. What we need to know first is the strategy of Satan. Satan used a certain strategy to drag down our first parents. He continues to use the same strategy to assault people today. Many are those who have fallen heavily without even knowing what has hit them! Many are those who realise that they are entangled in difficulties and conflicts of a spiritual nature, and do not know how to get out of them! We must understand the strategy of the devil, for smart though he is, his weapons are limited. He may appear to be so full of surprising moves and techniques, but his basic strategy may be understood from Genesis 3. His strategy consists of four main steps.

2.1   Catching You Unaware

The first step in Satan's strategy is to catch you unaware. You see him doing just that to Eve in Genesis 3. He appeared as a serpent and began talking to Eve. The serpent was one of the many creatures of God. Genesis 1:21 tells us that God created each creature "according to its kind". There were the elephants, the camels, the birds, and so on. There were probably different kinds of snakes that had been created by God.

Satan appeared as one of these snakes.

A snake can only hiss. On this occasion, that particular snake began to speak human words! This should have aroused Eve's suspicion. She should have put on her guard. She should have taken a step back, then another step, and run to her husband. And they should have run to God together for protection! In the Bible, there was only one other occasion when an animal spoke, and that was Balaam's ass. On that occasion, Balaam appeared to have been so annoyed to the point of failing to see the oddity of a donkey speaking. What could have accounted for Eve's want of suspicion?

We must understand that Eve was still in the state of innocency. She had not done anything wrong before, and there was a total absence of fear, shame or guilt in her. She was probably astounded when the snake began to speak, but she did not think that anything sinister could be hidden in that fact. The words of the serpent began to inform her mind. She began to think more of what was said by the serpent than of the oddity of the fact that it should speak. This was the beginning of her fall. She was caught totally unaware by the devil who was speaking through that snake. She was totally unaware that the devil had bad intentions upon her.

That continues to be Satan's approach today. He will attempt to catch you unaware. At the place where you least expect him to be present, there he will be! Just think – how would he catch you unaware today? Would he come to you as a snake and speak to you? Of course not! He knows that you would straightaway be on your guard. Would he then speak to you through the house lizard? Or through your dog, or cat? Of course not! Satan is not as foolish as that.

How then will he attack you? Let me tell you how. He will speak to you through men. He will speak to you through the mass media. He will attempt to change your thinking through false religions and philosophies. See how many people have been drawn away by the cults, by the religions invented by men, and by the so-called theory of evolution! "But these are respectable people whom we listen to," you might protest. But that is precisely the problem. The scientists are respectable people. The politicians are respectable people. So are the religious teachers, the news-readers and actors on television. And so are the advertisers and the people who attempt to get you to buy their goods, their cars and houses. These may be respectable people, but what we are saying is that through these people, Satan is attempting to draw you away from God and from anything that is spiritually helpful.

Remember that Satan was a mighty angel who was created by God. He rebelled against God and was cast to earth with those angels that followed him. The Bible calls him "the ruler of this world", and he will do all he can to capture as many people as possible and place them under his dominion. Satan is powerful! Satan is more subtle than you think. He will catch you at the point where you least expect him. Beware!

2.2   Attacks Indirectly

The next step taken by Satan is to attack you indirectly. In the garden of Eden, he came to Eve instead of to Adam. His real target was Adam, because Adam was the representative head of the human race. God did not make Eve, but Adam, the representative head. That was why the eyes of the two of them were not opened when Eve ate the fruit from the forbidden tree, but they were opened when Adam ate the fruit (vv. 6, 7). How would Adam have known that he was going to be attacked through Eve? He and Eve were the only two humans around at that time. Eve was Adam's wife, someone close to him – the "bone of his bones and flesh of his flesh". He would never have expected that Eve was going to be the instrument of his downfall!

Satan is a clever enemy. He will not come to you directly. He will get you 'hooked' through someone or something close to you. When he approached Eve, he asked Eve a question. Eve could have ignored him. She should have ignored him. You must never entertain Satan in any way. But Eve did just that. She replied to Satan's question. Satan wanted her to respond in some way. It would not have mattered if she had shouted back at him, or disagreed with him. All he wanted was for Eve to talk back to him in some way. It was very much like a fisherman who has thrown a line into the water. The fish comes, and then begins to examine the bait. All the fisherman wants is that the fish bites the bait. It does not matter from which direction the fish comes – whether from the left or the right, whether from the side or the bottom. It does not matter whether the fish pounces at the bait or gulps it down coolly. All the fisherman wants is that it bites the bait. The moment the fish bites, the hook will pierce through its mouth! That is all that the fisherman wants to happen! After that, he can take in the fish quickly or slowly. He can then boil it or fry it. Satan wants to get you hooked. He will do it indirectly!

Today, many people have been hooked by Satan. This has come about through their career, their health, recreation, or their children's education. Many are so caught up in their career that they have no time for anything else. Others are so caught up with some pursuit or other, such as nationalism, politics, or social issues, that they have no thought for their spiritual well-being. Others are too concerned about their health so that they invest too much time, money and energy in nutritional products, exercise and sports. There are those who are so concerned for their children's education that no thought is given to their own spiritual needs or that of their children. Think of the various extra lessons that you send your children to – extra tuition, piano lessons, ballet lessons, martial arts lessons, swimming lessons, mental arithmetic, computer classes, art classes,... The list appears endless! There is nothing wrong in sending them to some of these classes. It is good to have some other interests apart from studies. What is wrong is our obsession with them. We have come to think that these are in some ways indispensable. Our children's education seems to be what we live for. Look at the extent that some people go to in this area. They are prepared to sell their estates, their cars, their houses, and even migrate overseas, all for the sake of their children's education. They have failed to realise that, in the process, they are selling away their souls, and those of their children!

Is this not true? Think of the amount of money and time spent in giving the children a better education. Compare these with the effort made to meet their spiritual needs. Do you have family worship every evening? Do you teach your children the Bible? Do they learn to pray, and to memorise Scriptures? Do you pray often for their salvation? Many parents fall short in this area. They have been ensnared by the devil. Satan has attacked them indirectly, through their concern for the children's education, or through some other otherwise legitimate concerns!

Beware! Satan's intention is to get a hearing

from you. He wants to capture your attention. He wants you hooked. Once hooked, he will be able to lead you astray – slowly or quickly, imperceptibly or dramatically!

2.3 Questions The Word

The third step employed by the devil is to make you question the word of God. He will make you ask, Is the Bible really God's word? Is its teaching really true? Is it really sufficient to guide me in life? Is Jesus Christ alone the only way back to God? Surely there can't be any harm if I do this? Surely it would be all right if I don't do that? That was how he approached Eve. He came to Eve and asked, "Has God indeed said...?" He was actually sowing doubts into the mind of Eve about God's word.

Satan knows that the moment your faith in the Bible is undermined, your faith in God will also be shaken. He knows that once the Bible is not the authority in your life, errors of various kinds may be introduced easily. That is because the word of God is the basis of our faith. To have faith basically means to take God at His word. We believe because God has said it. The moment you lose confidence in God's word, that moment you lose confidence in God. Satan wants to accomplish precisely that. He wants you to trust God less, and less, and less... Of course, when your anchor is loosened up more and more, you will be easily moved away.

We have known of men who appeared to be so strong in their faith but are today in errors of various sorts. They shouted so loudly about their faith before, they spoke strongly about their views, but they were themselves not firmly anchored on the word of God. Their apparently strong views and opinions arose from reasons other than the fact that the Bible teaches those things. When confronted by clever and eloquent men, men with 'charisma', who sweet-talked to them, they succumbed! All their strongly-held views evaporated! They are today with those very people whom they used to oppose. It is all so saddening. Instead of changing for the better, they have turned worse. They are now with those who undermine the authority of the Bible, who utter so-called prophecies and claim to see visions. May God be merciful to them!

Do not be led away from believing what the Bible teaches. The Bible is God's word to man. Of course, you must ensure that those who appeal to the Bible are actually saying what the Bible teaches. We are, however, not too afraid of those who propagate falsehood by appealing to the Bible. When they direct people's attention to the Bible, the likelihood is that those who are sincere and sensible will discover soon enough their errors. No, we are more worried about those who draw you away from studying the Bible for yourself. Beware of this step in Satan's strategy!

2.4   Appeals To The Carnal Senses

The final step employed by the devil is to appeal to your carnal senses. You note how he did it to Eve. We are told in Genesis 3:6, "So when the woman saw that the tree was good for food, that it was pleasant to the eyes, and a tree desirable to make one wise, she took of its fruit and ate." Who would not want the fruit of that tree? It was "good for food", "pleasant to the eyes", "desirable to make one wise". But wait a moment before you stretch out your hand to pluck it! Does this not sound so familiar? Does it not remind us of the words of the apostle John? You would remember that he says in his first epistle, "For all that is in the world – the lust of the flesh, the lust of the eyes, and the pride of life – is not of the Father but is of the world (1 John 2:16)." That's it! The lust of the flesh, the lust of the eyes, and the pride of life! Satan will appeal to your carnal senses. He will attempt to trip you in that area.

Of course, Eve did not have the advantage of the words of the apostle John to help her. But she had God's words ringing in her ears. God had said to Adam and Eve, "In the day that you eat of it you shall surely die (Gen. 2:17)." Even in her state of innocency, she was tempted by her carnal senses. She found the fruit so appealing. She saw it as good for food, pleasing to the eyes, and good to make her wise. What would you have done in her place? Would you not have succumbed as well? And what with your fallen nature, would you not be more likely to fall?

Yes, many have fallen into the snare of the devil! Many have been burned by their sins. They have lacked self-control. They have ignored the warnings of God. They have bought that new car, that expensive dress, and so many things else, and ended up in debt. They have mixed with wrong company, and engaged in the lust of the flesh. Many have lost control of themselves, and done the thing that they now wish had never been done. "Oh, what a fool I have been!" But regret is too late. You have already fallen. All attempts to cover up your sin cannot erase the guilt in your conscience. You know that you have sinned against God! You have sinned!

That was how death came into the world. If Adam and Eve had not sinned against God, they would never have experienced physical death. And they would never have experienced spiritual death, which is separation from God. They would in all probability be translated to a higher level of glory in heaven, without the need to experience death and decay. However, they sinned, and brought death to the whole human race!

Today, Satan continues to ensnare the children of Adam and Eve. And he happily continues to employ the same strategy, perhaps with variations along the way, but it is basically the same strategy. The steps are the same. He would catch you unaware; he would attack you indirectly; he would cause you to question and doubt God's word; and he would appeal to your carnal senses. That accounts for the many falls that you have had. That explains the bitter experiences of many, and the absence of peace in your soul!

Three

Man's Folly

So when the woman saw that the tree was good for food, that it was pleasant to the eyes, and a tree desirable to make one wise, she took of its fruit and ate. She also gave to her husband with her, and he ate. (Genesis 3:6)

Why does Satan continue to use the same basic approach to ensnare people? The first reason is because his arsenal is limited in size. The number of weapons he has is limited. He cannot act differently from his nature. He will continue to lie, to use trickery, to murder souls. He is no doubt powerful, but God has put a limit to his power.

There is a second reason why he continues to use the same strategy. And that is that man cannot act contrary to his nature! Satan knows that! Man has inherited the same sinful, foolish nature from his parents. He continues to fall into the hand of Satan in the same basic way that Adam and Eve fell. Imagine how Satan must be laughing as one after another of the children of Adam falls in the same predictable way!

Just as there are four steps in Satan's strategy, there are four steps to man's tragedy.

3.1 Desiring Forbidden Knowledge

First, we note that man is so foolish in desiring forbidden knowledge all the time. It has been said that curiosity has killed more cats than the cats have killed rats. The same might be said of man. Curiosity has killed more souls than the souls have killed sins!

Consider what happened to Adam and Eve. Satan said to Eve, "You will not surely die. For God knows that in the day you eat of it your eyes will be opened, and you will be like God, knowing good and evil (Gen. 3:4-5)." Eve probably knew that Satan had gone too far in suggesting that God was trying to withhold something good from them. But her curiosity had been aroused. Her senses were tingling with life. She would not go so far as Satan to use the name of God, but she did think that the fruit would make her wise. She therefore ate the fruit, and passed it to her husband who also ate. You know what happened after that – the eyes of both of them were opened!

This is where we see the same trait in men today. We know the value of knowledge, and we teach our children to pursue knowledge. In the past, knowledge was pursued for its own sake, to make one wise. Knowledge was regarded as more precious than gold. Today, we continue to pursue knowledge, but it is no longer for its own sake. It is no longer done to make one wise. Instead, it is pursued in order to equip one to earn more money, and have a better life. Whatever the ultimate motive may be, we continue to pressure our children to pursue knowledge. And we have been doing so without any qualification added. We have failed to warn them that some knowledge is not worth having – that some knowledge is definitely harmful and should not be pursued at all.

We are warned in the Bible to flee from all forms of evil. There is, in fact, specific teaching about the need to avoid harmful and worthless knowledge. In 1 Corinthians 14:20, we are told, "Brethren, do not be children in understanding , however, in malice be babes, but in understanding be mature." Be mature! Do not be children in understanding. This is written in reference to things that are good, and right, and of spiritual benefit. But in things evil, be babes. Be as ignorant as you can about evil things. You see now how important it is to warn our children to avoid knowledge that is evil. Certain experiences in life are not worth having. Your friends in school may be boasting of their experiences in "chasing the dragon", which means to take drugs by inhaling their fumes. Experiences of that kind must be avoided, for it takes just one such experience to cause you to crave for more! By that stage, you are already hooked – addicted to the drug – and it will be extremely difficult to break away from it. Parents, warn your children about it! Teach them not to envy their friends, and never to succumb to their provocation. Avoid them!

Such experiences are certainly not worth having. Many are the people who today are smarting over their foolish exploits. They are suffering from a guilty conscience because of a particular incident that had occurred in their lives. They are regretting over the fact that they had lacked self-control. They had allowed curiosity to get the better of them. They had succumbed to their carnal desires. They had craved for forbidden knowledge, and they have been bitten! You know very well that that experience of yours had turned you into a different person from what you were before. You are not the better for it, but you have become worse off. Not all knowledge is useful or helpful!

Think of the child who is at home with her mother. Her mother says, "Child, stay here in this room while Mummy goes upstairs for a while. You may play with your toys or read your books. But do not open the window since it is night." Once the mother is upstairs, the child begins to wonder what it looks like outside the window. Curiosity gets the better of her. She places a chair below the window, unlatches it, and throws it open. To her great horror, she finds not a beautiful scene of mountains, blue sky and green trees, but utter darkness! She jumps as an owl hoots. She jumps again as a bat flies past. She cringes back in fear as a large moth lands on the window pane. She quickly slams the window shut, and trembles in terror. As her mother comes down she rushes to her, and clings to her, sobbing. "Mummy, I am frightened. It is so dark outside." "What have you done? Have you opened the window?" asks the mother. Of course she has! And she is that much the worse for it! Her life is now changed permanently. She is no longer the same as before. She now goes to bed fearing the dark. She has nightmares of owls hooting, bats flying, and moths landing before her face.

Is this not your experience? You have craved for forbidden knowledge. You have allowed curiosity to get the better of you. You have lacked self-control. You just couldn't stop yourself from experiencing the pleasures of the flesh... Oh, what a fall you have had! How you regret it now! But it is too late! Every time you are reminded of that past experience, you blush within yourself. You feel such a pang of shame and guilt coming over you. What others do not know, you know... And you know that God knows! That explains why you are so unhappy! That is why you feel the weight of sin upon your conscience!

3.2 Attempting To Cover Yourself

Man's foolishness is shown in another way – he attempts to cover up his own nakedness. When Adam and Eve discovered that they were naked, "they sewed fig leaves together and made themselves coverings (v. 7)." They probably chose the bigger leaves, and used twines to sew through the base of each leaf. They probably covered their lower waist, and their breast, and where else we do not know. They probably found that the leaves were so inadequate, for when the wind blew, they became exposed. They probably decided to sew also the ends of the leaves, but found that the leaves tore as a result of too much sewing. They probably had to sew new ones as before but the leaves were unable to keep them from the cold. Oh, foolish man and foolish woman! How can leaves be good enough for them?

You see that they were missing the point all together. It was not so much their physical nakedness that was the problem, for they had been naked before this and had not felt ashamed. It was after they had sinned against God that they knew shame..., and guilt..., and fear! Their problem was much worse than they had thought. It had to do more with their nature than with their physical nakedness. They had now a twisted and filthy nature, caused by their disobedience to God. Their good relationship with God was now severed. They had become enemies of God! Satan had scored a victory over them!

This is what has happened to you. You have a guilty conscience because of not obeying God. You have done what you knew to be wrong. You have acquired knowledge of the dark world. You are now reaping the fruit of your sins! And you are still trying to cover up your sins? All your attempts will fail! All your good works will not make up for your sins against God. All your attempts at righteous living will not be able to change your corrupt nature. It is useless trying to cover up your nakedness!

3.3   Hiding From God

There is another way by which man shows forth his foolishness – that is to try and hide himself from God.

God used to appear in the form of man and interacted closely with Adam and Eve. The appearance of God as man is called a 'theophany', i.e. 'a manifestation of God'. In a theophany, God assumed human form temporarily. This was in anticipation of the coming of the Son of God, who would take on human nature permanently. Jesus Christ is both God and Man, in one Person. Here, God appeared in the garden of Eden to seek out Adam and Eve. We are told in verse 8, "And they heard the sound of the Lord God walking in the garden in the cool of the day, and Adam and his wife hid themselves from the presence of the Lord God among the trees of the garden."

That is what sinful men and women, and boys and girls, continue to do. Like creatures of the dark, they scatter at the first appearance of light. They are unable to bear the slightest amount of light. It hurts their eyes. It exposes their filth. But it is foolish to run away from the light. We are not meant for living in darkness. We are made to have fellowship with God – to glorify Him and to enjoy Him forever. Yes, it is a fact that you have fallen. It is a fact that you have badly hurt yourself and cannot cure yourself. But why should you be running away from the only person who can do you good? Why not come to God and face the consequences of your sins? Why not cast yourself upon Him for mercy? You remember how David sinned against God and was confronted by the prophet Gad with three alternative punishments. What was David's reply? He said, on that occasion, "I am in great distress. Please let us fall into the hand of the

Lord, for His mercies are great; but do not let me fall into the hand of man (2 Sam. 24:14)." David was very wise in his choice. He knew that he could not escape from the punishment of God, for God is just and has to punish all sins. But he knew at the same time that God is merciful, and it was far better to fall into *His* hand than into the hand of man.

Do you have such a conception of God? Do you realise that God is full of mercy and pity towards sinners like you and me? You would remember the parable of the prodigal son. The wasteful son squandered all that he had and ended up desiring pig-food. When he came to an end of himself, when he could do nothing else to help himself, he thought of his father's home. He decided to return, although with so much fear and trembling. There he is, dragging himself home in such a pathetic manner! And what do you think the father is like? Is he angry and fuming, waiting to beat up his son, to disown him and drive him away? You know the story! The father is longing for His son's return. He is peering into the distance, and he catches sight of his son! He quickly runs down the road to his son, falls on his neck and kisses him. Oh, friend, our Father in heaven longs for your return to Him!

But see how foolish the sinner is! He is trying to hide himself from God. That is why God takes the initiative to seek out the sinner. God came to Adam and Eve and asked, "Where are you?", "What have you done?" It wasn't that God did not know where they were and what they had done. God is all-knowing. His purpose of confronting them with these questions was to awaken them to their senses, to make them acknowledge their guilt, and to cause them to trust Him in order to be saved.

It is foolish of sinners to try and hide themselves from God.

3.4   Doubting God's Solution

Man shows forth his folly in another way – that is, to doubt that God has the solution to his problem. Remember that your sin is against God. You have lost the right to be in friendship with Him. Nothing you do will be able to put the situation right. In His mercy, God has revealed to us His solution to our problem. He has shown that a life must be laid down in the place of the sinner so that he might live. Blood must be shed for the cleansing of his sins. A sacrifice is needed in order that the sinner might be forgiven. This is in order that the justice of God might be fulfilled. God must punish sin. He has arranged for a Saviour to be punished on behalf of the sinner so that the sinner may go free.

This, God reveals in verse 21, "Also for Adam and his wife the Lord God made tunics of skin, and clothed them." An animal was put to death for the first time. The skin of the animal was made into proper coats to cover up their nakedness. These were certainly better than the coverings of leaves that they had made. Adam and Eve did not have to feel cold any more. And their nakedness was now covered up.

We must note that there is a deeper message than that. God was not only covering up their physical nakedness. He was actually teaching Adam and Eve that from that time on, they had to approach Him by way of animal sacrifices. The system of animal sacrifices practised by all who would approach God was introduced at that time. It did not begin with the time of Moses. Moses only began putting down in writing what had been practised all along by generations of people who worshipped the true God.

The system of animal sacrifices was to point man to the Saviour, the Lord Jesus Christ. He was revealed in due time as the Lamb of God who takes away the sin of the world. But man finds this hard to believe. He continues to doubt and reject the solution that God has provided. Today, we continue trying to cover our own nakedness in our own way. We hide ourselves away from the God who alone can save us. And when God's solution to our problem is revealed to us, we doubt its efficacy. We question its effectiveness. We want to rely on our own wisdom and ability to save ourselves.

That is why God has to deal with each one of us in a certain way, to awaken us to our senses!

Four

God's Remedy

And I will put enmity between you and the woman, and between your seed and her Seed; He shall bruise your head, and you shall bruise His heel. (Gen. 3:15)

Left to ourselves, there will be no hope for us. We have fallen to Satan's strategy. We have sinned against God. We are unable to save ourselves from the consequences of sin.

God has mercifully taken the initiative to provide us the way of salvation. He comes to fallen man with *His* remedy! His remedy consists of four steps. If you are to be saved, you will have to be dealt with by Him in these four steps.

4.1 Exposing Your Sins

First, God has to expose your sins. He will come to you and search you out, just as He searched out Adam. God called out to Adam, asking, "Where are you?" God knew where Adam had hidden himself. He asked the question only to engage Adam's attention. He wanted Adam to know that he was being spoken to personally.

In the same way, God searches out His people today. He knows that sinners will instinctively run, and hide themselves from Him. But where can you run to? Where can you hide? Remember that God is God. He is all-knowing and all-powerful. You are merely a creature of His. He knows everything about you, and all that you have done. Nothing is hidden from Him. Then, you must remember that the whole universe belongs to Him. He created all things, and everything is under His control. He needs only to say the word and the earth will reveal where you have hidden yourself. He can easily stretch out His fingers to pick you out from any mouse-hole.

It is useless trying to hide yourself from God. God speaks to individuals through their Christian friends, through the reading of a book, or through hearing the Bible explained. In a meeting where many people are gathered to hear the Bible explained, God speaks personally to the hearers. If you are present in such a meeting, God might single you out to speak to you personally. The words of the preacher might be addressed to the many people present at the meeting, but you know that God is speaking to you personally. In the same way, God may be speaking to you now. Not everyone in the world will read this booklet. You are one of those who read it. God is speaking to you through the pages of this booklet. You may replace Adam's name with yours and apply the words to yourself – "Where are you?"

God asked Adam more questions. In verse 11, we have the questions: "Who told you that you were naked? Have you eaten from the tree of which I commanded you that you should not eat?" Again, it was not that God did not know. He already knew the answers to those questions. His purpose of asking those questions was to expose Adam's sin. He wanted Adam to admit his sin. Like any fallen man, Adam was so good at justifying himself, and blaming others. He tried to push the blame to his wife. Of course, God had to deal with Eve as well. That was why He turned to Eve and asked, "What is this you have done?" (v. 13). This only underlines the truth that God deals with each person individually. He dealt with Adam, and He dealt with Eve. It is useless to defend yourself and give excuses for your sins. It is useless trying to hide what you have done. God does not have to wait for a little bird to come and tell Him what you have done. He does not have to wait for a little ant to whisper to Him what it has seen. God is all-knowing.

He already knows!

4.2   Exposing Your Useless Efforts

Next, God has to expose the uselessness of your efforts at saving yourself. You need to understand the seriousness of your sins. You have sinned against light. You have broken God's law. You have sinned against God Himself! What can you do to change the situation?

Some people try out religion. Others trust in living a principled life. Yet others try to appease their stricken conscience with good works of various kinds. Some channel their energy to providing their children a good life. In the process, they indulge them with so much that is unnecessary and even harmful. Others bury themselves in their work and become "workaholics". Some would engage themselves in sports or other recreation to keep happy. But all the happiness they get is only temporary. You know that your basic problems remain unsolved.

Consider how big your problems are. First, there is the fallen human nature that needs to be changed. Can you change the spots on a leopard, or the stripes on a tiger? You know it is impossible to change human nature. We are talking about your *nature*, not just your body. You can alter how you look by plastic surgery, but you cannot make clean your nature by surgery of any kind.

Secondly, there are your sins to be atoned for. You have caused offence to God. God's holy anger now rests on you. There is enmity between you and God. How may that state of enmity be removed? How may you be reconciled to Him? How can God be a Friend to you so that you may be received by Him? The fact is that no amount of good works and good intentions can make up for the wrong you have done to God.

Thirdly, you have to have a certain righteousness before you can enter heaven. All of us wish to go to heaven. None of us wants to go to hell. Let us assume for a moment that your sinful nature has been made clean and the enmity between you and God has been cancelled. You are now taken to heaven. You will discover that it is impossible for you to survive in heaven because everything there is righteous but you are not. You will be like a diver who has not the diving suit nor the right equipment to survive in the deep ocean. What you need is the suit of righteousness that God alone can provide, through His Son, Jesus Christ!

Be clear about this – your problems are essentially spiritual in nature. Nothing done in the physical realm, in a physical way, can alter what is essentially spiritual. Unlike a mountain which has dimensions of height, length and breath, your problems are without such dimensions. A high mountain can still be scaled. A thick mountain can still be dug through by modern equipment. But nothing can be done to overcome the problems that we have just talked about. The reason is that your problems are spiritual in nature. They are of such colossal proportions as to be proportionless! It will be easier to scoop out the ocean than to change your sinful nature, or to turn away God's holy anger, or to weave a cloak of righteousness for yourself.

You are naked before God!

4.3 Exposing You To His Solution

The third thing God wishes to do is to expose you to *His* solution to your problems. He reveals to us in verse 15 that a particular Seed, or Descendant, of the woman will be the Saviour of the world. This Saviour was in due time revealed to be none other than Jesus Christ. He would act as the Mediator between God and man.

You would surely know what a mediator is. In many parts of the world, people still depend on a mediator to help when there is a quarrel. He acts as the middle person, to bring the two parties together so that they will be on talking terms again. The best mediator is someone who knows the two parties well, and is trusted by both parties. In the business world, a middle person is often needed before a transaction is sealed. He acts as a business consultant, who knows the needs of one party and the products of another party. He matches the needs to the products, taking into consideration the use of those products, the budget, the specifications, and various other considerations. You would not want to be swindled in a business deal. You would need a competent and reliable business consultant, a good mediator.

Jesus Christ is the Mediator between God and man. He is actually the second person of the Godhead. He is God, who came to take on human nature. He is therefore God and Man at the same time. He has two natures in one person. Being divine, He represents God perfectly. Being human, and without sin, He represents man perfectly. He is the perfect Mediator between God and fallen man. No better Mediator can be found apart from Christ. No other Saviour there is apart from Him!

Not only is the person of the Saviour revealed, but His work as well. We are told that He will bruise the serpent's head, while being bruised by the serpent in His heel. This is a reference to the destruction of Satan's power by the death of Christ on the cross.

The head is the centre of power. When the head is crushed, the whole body is rendered useless. That is why in a war, one party will seek to strike at the enemy's headquarters, or to kill the commander-in-chief. Satan knew the importance of striking at the head. He struck at Adam, the representative head of the human race. God, however, raised up another Head to save sinners. Satan struck at Him as well, causing Him to die on the cross. Death is the last stronghold of Satan, but it was unable to hold back the Saviour. Jesus Christ rose from death, and defeated Satan. That is what is meant by, "He will bruise your head, and you shall bruise His heel." Satan's head was bruised in his attempt to destroy the Saviour.

All the animal sacrifices offered by worshippers in the Old Testament time, beginning with Adam, were meant to point to the person and work of Christ. A life had to be laid down in order that the worshipper may have eternal life. Blood had to be shed for the cleansing of his sins. A sacrifice had to be offered to turn away God's holy anger from the sinner. The animal sacrifices of the Old Testament time were, by themselves, unable to accomplish all these. They only pointed to Jesus Christ, who finally came to offer Himself up as the necessary and sufficient sacrifice to God. That is why you are commanded by God to turn from your sins and to trust in Christ alone for salvation.

4.4   Exposing Satan's Desire To Destroy You

There is a fourth, and final, step in God's remedy – that is, to expose Satan's desire to destroy you! Satan knew of God's intention to provide a Saviour for sinners. God had revealed that there will be enmity between the serpent and the woman, between the serpent's seed and the woman's Seed.

That enmity began to unfold itself in the drama of history. The Bible tells us that there are two groups of people in this world – those who are the children of God, and those who are the children of the devil. The children of the devil will always be at enmity with the children of God. The seed of the serpent had always attempted to destroy the seed of the woman with the intention of cutting off the godly line. If the godly line could be cut off there would have been no possibility of the coming of that particular Seed of the woman, Jesus Christ. God's plan of saving for Himself a people would have been frustrated.

The Bible actually shows that there were a number of occasions when Satan almost succeeded in cutting off the godly line. Each time, however, God ensured that the godly line was continued. At last, when the appointed time had arrived, the Saviour was born into the world. Satan made one desperate attempt to destroy the Saviour. That occasion was when Herod ordered all infant boys of two years and below to be killed. Joseph and Mary, having been forewarned by an angel, brought the infant Jesus to Egypt. They remained there until it was safe to return to Palestine. Jesus Christ grew up, appeared in public, and was killed on the cross of Calvary.

Satan thought that he had finally destroyed the Saviour when Jesus Christ died. Christ, however, rose from death and in that way destroyed the power of Satan. His death was, at the same time, an offering to God on behalf of His people. His blood was shed for the cleansing of their sins, exactly as God had intended! You see now how Satan was outwitted! You understand now why Satan is raging like a roaring lion, intending to destroy as many of God's people as possible. There was enmity between the children of Satan and the children of God before the time of Christ. That enmity continues after Christ has come. If anything, Satan is more angry than before! He will do his worst before his own doom comes.

This is where everyone needs to take heed. Satan is a defeated foe. Christ has broken his power. He is in his death throes. He can still cause a lot of damage, and is extremely dangerous. He knows that the time will come when he will be thrown into the torments of eternal hell. He will therefore do his utmost to cause Christians to stumble, and deny the faith. Believers will be the target of his attacks.

By the same token, he will attempt to prevent others from coming to faith in Jesus Christ. He will sow doubts into your mind. He will cause dullness of understanding so that you cannot see spiritual truths. He will bring opposition into your life to prevent you from hearing more of God's word. He will attempt to lure you away by the cults, or in some subtle ways prevent you from coming to faith in Christ. Be warned of Satan's strategy!

God has revealed His solution to our problems. He has also warned us of Satan's intention to destroy as many people as possible. Beware of Satan! Do not allow him to hinder you from coming to Christ!

Five

Over To You!

An ancient document is valued only by those who know its worth. The third chapter of Genesis has been preserved for the benefit of those who would value it. It is an ancient document with a relevant message to modern man.

It reveals how our first parents fell from their standing before God into sin, and how God mercifully saved them. It gives us an insight into our problems and how these may be overcome. Man's problems are of a spiritual nature. They cannot be solved by mere human effort. God has intervened so that there may be a way out of our problems.

Very soon, life as we know it now will be over. Jesus Christ will return to judge the world. Every soul will be resurrected, to join those who are still alive on earth. Everyone will be given a new body. The separation of the righteous from the wicked will occur. Those who are not clothed with Christ's righteousness will be thrown into hell, to suffer eternal damnation with Satan and the wicked demons. The universe will be melted down and made new. Those who are clothed in Christ's righteousness will dwell with the holy God for ever and ever...

Dear Reader, do you still doubt the message contained in Genesis 3? Do you still doubt that Satan is actively employing his strategy to ensnare people? Do you doubt that your problems should be attributed to your fall into his hand? Do you doubt the reality of Satan's existence? Beware! If you doubt Satan's existence, you also doubt God's existence! Satan is as real as God. If God exists, Satan also exists! And if Satan exists, you can be sure that he will be actively attempting to sow doubts into your mind!

There has been enough spiritual interest to keep you reading up to this point. Do not allow Satan to rob you of this last ounce of interest. Do not allow him to take away the little belief left in you. Turn to God to seek mercy from Him! If Satan has his strategy, God has His remedy! His remedy, as we have seen, is the person and work of Christ. Jesus Christ has done everything necessary to save sinners from sin, from Satan, from eternal damnation in hell. Christ has offered Himself up on the cross of Calvary for His people. His blood has been shed for the cleansing of their sins. His life has been laid down in order that you may have life.

Turn, therefore, from your sins and seek peace with God through faith in Jesus Christ!

Other books by the same author:

1 A BASIC CATECHISM OF THE CHRISTIAN FAITH

2 A GARDEN ENCLOSED: A Historical Study And Evaluation Of The Form Of Church Government Practised By The Particular Baptists In The 17th And 18th Centuries.

3 AGAINST PARITY: A Response To The Parity View Of The Church Eldership

4 A MULTIFACETED JEWEL: Studies on the Local Church

5 CESSATIONISM OR CONTINUATIONISM?: An Exposition of 1 Corinthians 12-14 and Related Passages

6 FLEE ALSO YOUTHFUL LUSTS: An Exposition of 2 Timothy 2:22

7 INDEPENDENCY: THE BIBLICAL FORM OF CHURCH GOVERNMENT

8 TAMING JACOB: How A Restless Soul Found Peace With God

9 THE FUNDAMENTALS OF OUR FAITH: Studies On The 1689 Baptist Confession Of Faith

10 THE HIDDEN LIFE: A Call To Discipleship

11 THE KEYS OF THE KINGDOM: A Study On The Biblical Form Of Church Government

12 THE ROSE OF SHARON, THE LILY OF THE VALLEYS: An Exposition on the Song of Solomon

13 THE CHRISTIAN IN THE CHINESE CULTURE

14 THOROUGHGOING REFORMATION: What It Means To Be Truly Reformed

15 WHAT IS A REFORMED BAPTIST CHURCH?

16 WORLD MISSIONS TODAY: A Theological, Exegetical, and Practical Perspective Of Missions